Emily Brontë: A real Life Heroine

Bobbi Taudel-Maddox

Emily Brontë: A Real Life Heroine

"[...] no amount of fact can give flesh to Emily Brontë's character" (Hardwick, 17). Emily Brontë lived an imaginative, yet emotionally scaring childhood. From here, she carried her creativity through her seculsive adulthood, creating a novel which told her life story in a twisted reality. Emily's poetry also reveals her life's story through the "Gondal Chronicles". Her wish for death was granted through consumption, which was never tended to due to her own negligence. Although Emily Brontë had written only one novel, through her life, poems, and Wuthering Heights she has become a real life heroine.

Emily Brontë was born on July 30th, 1818 in Thornton, near Bradford, Yorkshire, making her the fifth child in the Brontë family. She had three sisters before her: Maria, Elizabeth, and Charlotte, and then there was her brother Branwell. Then on January 17th, 1820, Emily received another sister, Anne. Shortly after the birth of Anne, the Brontë family moved to Haworth, establishing themselves there in April of 1820. This is where the true story of Emily's life is formed. Only a short year later, Emily's mother, Maria, died. It was September 15th, 1821, when the consumption stole her away from her six children that she delivered in seven years. Maria's sister, Elizabeth Branwell, moved in with the rest of the Brontë family to help Patrick (Emily's father) take care of the children. Patrick, being the incumbent of Haworth, was strict yet loving. He felt education and knowledge were the most important features in a person's life. "Patrick encouraged his children in their pursuit of knowledge. Any books that came their way were eagerly devoured [...]" (The Brontë's Personage and Family History). This is where Emily's education started. In November of 1824, Emily, now age six, was enrolled in the Clergy Daughter's School at Cowan Bridge. Her education here was short lived. After six months of being away at school, she had to return home. Her sister, Maria, fell ill and died on May 6th, 1825. Charlotte and Emily came home to help their family cope and survive. Unfortunately, Elizabeth, the second eldest sister, fell ill as well. She died a month after Maria, on June 1ˢᵗ, 1825. These deaths were devastating to Emily. Emily's nature started to become withdrawn and peculiar. "My sister's disposition was not naturally gregarious; circumstances favoured and fostered her tendency to seclusion; except to go to church or take a walk on the hills, she rarely crossed the threshold of home" (Brontë, vi). Emily clung to her sisters and brother for companionship. She kept herself contained, creating a small, narrow life for herself.

Figure 1: Emily, Charlotte, and Anne; The Brontë Society

Emily's oral literature and imaginative writings with Anne stemmed from these times and Charlotte's games. In June of 1826, Patrick Brontë brought home twelve wooden soldiers for Branwell.

"Branwell, came to our door with a box of soldiers, Emily and I jumped out of bed and I snatched up one and exclaimed this is the Duke of Wellington it shall be mine!" (Brontë, 1056). The soldiers became the basis of the Brontë children's fantasy world. Their writings became the Angria story, where they acted out parts from the Duke of Wellington, and his sons, Charles and Arthur Wellesley. Charlotte contrived the idea that each sibling should create, manage, and own his/her own island. Each child named his/her island after heroic leaders. Charlotte created Wellington, Branwell invented Sneaky, Emily created Perry, and Anne invented Ross. The time passing, imaginative games created Emily and Anne into true writers. When Emily became tired of Charlotte's antics, she seized Anne as her partner and began the Gondal Saga. However, before her poetry became her main focus, Emily attempted traditional school again, attending the Roe Head School in Dewsbury. Unfortunately, for the seventeen year old, Emily fell ill to a bout of homesickness after only three months. Anne took her place at the school. This added to Emily's seclusion.

By this point, she barely had friends and barely left home. To make matters worse, she also had no manners, no positive disposition, and no feminine behavior.

"Our school-scheme has been abandoned and instead Charlotte and I went to Brussels on the 8th of February 1842 [...] I returned from Brussels November 8th 1842 in consequence to Aunt's Death [...]" ~ Emily Brontë's Diary Entry July 30, 1845

Emily's lack of poise did not stop her from attempting to follow her dreams. In September of 1838, she went to Law Hill School to teach. Emily was working seventeen hours a day, which caused her body to physically break down. She left after seven months, returning home in April of 1839. Once again, in hopes of becoming more educated, Emily attended school in Brussels with Charlotte in February of 1842. Here, she studied foreign languages, writing essays in French, and continued her musical

Figure 2: Aunt Branwell; The Brontë Society

studies as well. During this time, her Aunt Branwell fell ill, and died in November of 1842. Emily returned home for the last time, never to venture out again. She became "a woman of remarkable force of character, reserved and taciturn" (Cousin, 1188). Emily finally grew into the serious, wounded, fragile, and suffering woman that is known today. However, this became the high point of Emily's life, leading into her creative and imaginative writing period. She began to compile her poetry in 1844, only to be discovered by Charlotte in October of 1845. Charlotte convinced Emily and Anne, Emily's writing partner, to publish their poems. During the publishing process, Emily began to write *Wuthering Heights*, her only novel, which took her a total of seven months to complete (December 1845 – July 1846). Following the completion of *Wuthering Heights*, Emily wrote her last poem ever on September 14th, 1846 "Emily's voice disappeared" (Hardwick, 18). She was living a life of misery between her father, who was dealing with dystonia and blindness, her brother, who was a jobless, loveless drunk, and her two sisters, who either could not or would not care about Branwell. "[…] Branwell worse than helpless; yet, with ever-increasing expenses and no earnings, bare living difficult to compass. The future, too, was uncertain; should their father's case prove hopeless, should he become quite blind, ill, incapable of work, they would be homeless indeed" (Robinson, 1884). With this in mind, Emily sent *Wuthering Heights* off to be published. She succeeded in July of 1847 - however, the response from the critics was not what she was expecting.

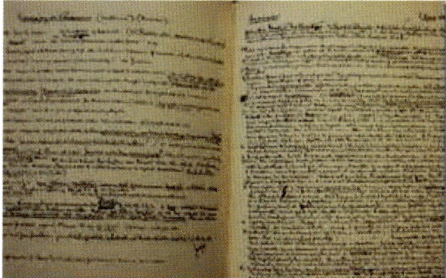

Figure 3: Emily's Diary; The Brontë Society

Emily's only novel, *Wuthering Heights*, was originally part of a set of books, three volumes long, The first two volumes were comprised of *Wuthering Heights* and the third volume was written by her sister, Anne, called *Agnes Gray*. Emily published her book under the pseudonym Ellis Bell with Anne as Acton Bell. Her book was not accepted as superior achievement at first, receiving mixed reviews and much controversy. Reviewers of the time stated the book was "a disagreeable story", "gloomy and dismal", and "a purposeless power". One reviewer even stated, "We know nothing in the whole range of our fictitious literature which represents such shocking pictures of the worst forms of humanity" (The Reader's Guide to Emily Brontë's *Wuthering Heights*). Even her own sister, Charlotte, condemned it for its amoral passion. She reedited the book after Emily's death and published it as a standalone novel in 1850 under Emily's real name. Although Charlotte had the best intentions, she cursed the novel herself. "Whether it is right or advisable to create beings like Heathcliff, I do not know: I scarcely think it is" (Brontë, ix). However, Charlotte continues to explain to the reader, "To all such *Wuthering Heights* must appear a rude and strange production [....] Be the work grim or glorious, dread or divine, you have little choice left but to quiescent adoption" (Brontë, v-ix). Making the readers want to read the novel and discover what Charlotte is referring to, therefore she did Emily justice. In today's world, *Wuthering Heights* is a classic of English literature described as being "close to the regressive, to the anarchy of instinct. *Wuthering Heights* has a sustained brilliance and originality we hardly know how to account for" (Hardwick, 6-31). Emily created a gothic novel in the height of the romantic period, subjecting herself to ridicule stemming from Charlotte's *Jane Eyre*. However different or opposite her novel is, Emily wrote about what she knew about connecting her family and place of home into every inch of the novel.

Looking at the location of the two homes in the novel, Wuthering Heights and Thrushcross Grange, are clearly a part of the real place Emily grew up in. Throughout the novel, Emily speaks about Heathcliff and Catherine running across the moors. She paints these pictures quite well because Emily spent most of her life running across the moors in Haworth.

Figure 4: The Moors; *A Reader's Guide to Wuthering Heights*

These moors consisted of miles and miles of grassy land. In chapter four of the novel, Mr. Earnshaw begins the story of Heathcliff by journeying to Liverpool from Wuthering Heights; he claims this trip is sixty miles long. When mapping Haworth to Liverpool, the real trip is approximately sixty-three miles long. This is not the only geographically correct location in the novel either. The house itself, Wuthering Heights, appears to be based off of Top Withens.

Figure 5: Top Withens: *A Reader's Guide to Wuthering Heights*

Although the layout of the house is not the same, the location of it compares to the Heights. It is isolated and windswept. Taking the location of Top Withens and combining it with High Sunderland Hall, a building Emily became familiar with while working at Law Hill School, and the whole picture of Wuthering Heights is formed.

Figure 6: Sunderland Hall; *A Reader's Guide to Wuthering Heights*

The latter is the layout of the Heights. Along with these two physical inspirational buildings, Emily created Thrushcross Grange from Ponden Hall, another building Emily was much acquainted with.

Figure 7: Ponden Hall; *A Reader's Guide to Wuthering Heights*

The last true inspiration for locations in *Wuthering Heights* was Ponden Kirk. This out crag of rock lies approximately one kilometer north from Top Withens. Ponden Kirk is the real life location of Penistone Crags. This area is noted in chapter eighteen, when Catherine learns about the fairy cave. Ponden Kirk has a hole in the bottom of its structure, which would be the opening to this fairy cave. "It was not her lack of knowledge of the world that made the novel she wrote become *Wuthering Heights*, nor her inexperience, but rather her experience, limited and perverse, indeed, and specialized by a most singular temperament, yet close and very real" (Robinson, 1982). Emily not only used her experience of physical locations for her novel, but her experiences of people as well.

Figure 8: Ponden Kirk; *A Reader's Guide to Wuthering Heights*

Figure 9: Sir Laurence Olivier as Heathcliff; *A Reader's Guide to Wuthering Heights*

Emily created a strange, bizarre hero: Heathcliff, portrayed by Sir Laurence Olivier in the 1939 movie. He was a man who was careless, hard, destructive, and self-indulgent. Heathcliff is famously known by his beginning description and introduction in the novel.

He is a dark-skinned gypsy in aspect, in dress and manners a gentleman: that is as much a gentleman as many a country squire: rather slovenly, perhaps, yet not looking a miss with his negligence, because

he has an erect and handsome figure; rather morose

[....] He'll love and hate equally under cover, and

esteem it a species of impertinence to be loved or

hated again (Brontë, 3).

This is the first look the reader gets of Heathcliff and throughout the rest of the novel the vision never seems to change. He is constantly referred to as "dirty", "ragged", and "low ruffian". The reader sees this cruel man the same way Charlotte saw him, "[…] he was a child neither of Lascar or gypsy, but a man's shape animated by demon life – a ghoul – an afreet" (Brontë, viii). Heathcliff is judged harshly by most readers and as the story progresses these judgments get harsher. "Heathcliff, indeed, stands unredeemed; never once swerving in his arrow – straight course to perdition […] the single link that connects Heathcliff with humanity is his rudely confessed regard for Hareton Earnshaw […] than his half-implied esteem for Nelly Dean" (Brontë, viii). With such a character, where did Emily ever discover the idea from?

**Figure 10: Branwell drawing;
The Brontë Society**

Emily's phantoms came directly from her own home, her own blood, Branwell. Branwell led a tragic, depressing life of his own, despite his father's encouragement to rise to a high stature in society. Branwell started his misguided path young in life. He was supposed to study painting in London at the Academy Schools. However, he was a failure. He did not attend school and spent his time drinking at the taverns instead. "His nature was hysterical, addictive, self-indulgent. Very early he fell under the spell of alcohol and opium; his ravings and miseries destroyed the family peace, absorbed their energies, and depressed their spirits" (Hardwick, 4). Emily, unlike her sisters, continued to have compassion for Branwell, always wanting to protect him and remaining sympathetic to him. Unfortunately, Branwell continued to destroy his family and his own health, leading to his death at age thirty-one. Prior to his death and during the process of the novel, "[…] Emily drew heavily on him for the memorable portrait of Heathcliff in *Wuthering Heights*. Branwell […] served his sister Emily, not indeed as a model, a thing to copy, but as a chart of proportions by which to measure, and to which to refer, for correct investiture, the inspired idea" (Robinson, 2034). Branwell's bitterness, frustration, and violence are found at Heathcliff's core.

Heathcliff and Branwell were both self-indulgent, violent, and quite bitter throughout their lives. Their childhood is them to this fate. Branwell being the least successful of the Brontë children and

Heathcliff being the least wanted of the Earnshaw children. "He was not insolent to his benefactor, he was simply insensible; though knowing perfectly the hold he had on his heart, and conscious he had only to speak and all the house would be obliged to bend to his wishes" (Brontë, 32). Regardless of their childhoods, both in some form, had companions who cared for them: Branwell had Emily, his biological sister, and Heathcliff had Catherine, his adopted sister. Both men went through some type of schooling and both failed. Branwell went away and became a drunk where as Heathcliff just could not keep up with Catherine, whether he cared to or not.

> In the first place, he had by that time lost the benefit of his early education: continual hard work, begun soon and concluded late, had extinguished and curiosity he once possessed in pursuit of knowledge, and any love for books or learning [....] He struggled long to keep up an equality with

• • •

Catherine in her studies, […] he took a grim pleasure, apparently in exciting the aversion rather than the esteem of his few acquaintance (Brontë, 57).

School was not the only commonality both Branwell and Heathcliff had; they also struggled with love. Branwell had fallen in love with a married woman. This woman's husband banished Branwell from ever seeing her again. This story remains true for Heathcliff and Catherine, years after her marriage to Edgar and once Heathcliff returned to the Heights. Branwell, like Heathcliff, swore his love for the woman was much more than her husband could give her. Branwell was rude and moody in the writings that he created at the same time *Wuthering Heights* was being created. "Looking at a letter Branwell wrote, he said, "My own life without her would be hell. What can the so-called love of her wretched sickly husband be to her compared with mine?" (Robinson, 2053). Then looking at Heathcliff's reaction to Catherine's marriage, he states, "Two words would comprehend my future – death and hell; existence after losing her would be hell. Yet I was a fool to fancy for a moment that she valued Edgar Linton's attachment more than mine. If he loved with all the powers of his puny being, he couldn't love in eighty years as much as I could in a day" (Brontë, 128). This lack of love, cruelty, and misery led Branwell and Heathcliff down a path of loneliness. Emily tried to fill this void for Branwell by caring for him the way a wife would. "She was not his wife, but she had to serve him as only a loyal partner can do when the normal barriers of common civility have broken down" (Gérin, 244). Emily loved Branwell the way Catherine Earnshaw loved Heathcliff and took care of him the way Catherine (Linton) Heathcliff (Cathy) took care of Heathcliff. Cathy once stated to Heathcliff, "You are miserable, are you not? Lonely, like the devil, and envious like him? Nobody loves you – nobody will cry for you when you die! I wouldn't be you!" (Brontë, 247), but she refused to leave his house, the same way Emily refused to leave Branwell. "Emily appears to have seen his case with perfect lucidity; he could not benefit by any renunciation of hers, he was beyond rescuing, but she refused to abandon him" (Gérin, 244). Emily's love for Branwell aided her in creating Heathcliff and his companion Catherine.

Catherine Earnshaw, Heathcliff's love, and Catherine (Linton) Heathcliff (Cathy), Heathcliff's form of revenge, have one major similarity: they both are pieces of Emily. There is only one other major similarity between the two: they both have compassion for Heathcliff, just like Emily. "It is, indeed, central to the conception of Heathcliff that his creator viewed him with more compassion than hate" (Gérin, 219). This compassion stems from the fact that Heathcliff is Branwell. Therefore, Emily used both heroines of her novel to represent herself.

Figure 11: Merle Oberon as Catherine (Earnshaw) Linton; *A Reader's Guide to Wuthering Heights*

In the first volume, or the first half, of *Wuthering Heights*, Catherine (Earnshaw) Linton, portrayed by Merle Oberon in the 1939 movie, is the heroine. Catherine is a true piece of Emily. The first description the reader gets of Catherine is, "A wild, wicked slip she was - but she had the bonniest and lightest foot in the parish: and after all I believe she ment no harm; [...]" (Brontë, 35).

Catherine, as a child, was bored and restless, which is what led her to always run wild on the moors. Emily had the same nature as a child. "The sharpness of her tongue, [...] were only equal by her warm heart and generous nature" (Gérin, 7). Emily painted an image of herself in Catherine, who, once she received Heathcliff, played with him like a toy. "She was much too fond of Heathcliff. The greatest punishment we could intvent for her was to keep her seperate from him [...]" (Brontë, 35). Like Emily with Branwell, Catherine always wanted to be with Heathcliff. Even when she left the house, she would drag him along to enjoy the outting. "But it was one of their chief amusements to run away to the moors in the morning [...]" (Brontë, 38). Catherine loved to be wild on the moors like Emily. There also came a point, a turning point in Catherine's life that changed her.

> Cathy stayed at Thrushcross Grange five weeks: till Christmas [....] The mistress [...] commenced her plan of reform by trying to raise her self-respect

● ● ●

with fine clothes and flattery, which she too readily;
so that, instead of a wild, hatless little savage
jumping into the house, and rushing to squeeze us
all breathless, there lighted from a handsome black
pony a very dignifid person [....] [she looked] like a
lady now (Brontë, 43).

Catherine became lady-like, growing up in a short amount of time.
Emily went through a similar situation, going away to school and
returning home because of the death of her sister, Maria, which
forced her to grow up. As Catherine grew older, she became
nostalgic for her childhood. She also grew hard, careless,
destructive, and self-indulgent. Catherine, except for Heathcliff,
truly cared only about herself. She had plenty of people around
her, yet chose to be lonely. "[...] can't make yourself content!"
(Brontë, 65). Catherine could never make herself happy or content
no matter what choices she made. Emily secluded herself in life,
like Catherine. She had family and friends around, but this could

never make her truly happy.

> I am bound to vow that she had scarcely more
> practical knowledge of the peasentry amoungst
> whom she lived, than a nun has of the country
> people who sometimes pass through her convent
> gates [....] Though her feeling for the people round
> as benevolent, intercourse with them she never
> sought; nor, with very few exceptions, ever
> experienced. And yet she knew them: knew their
> ways, their language, their family histories; she
> could hear of them with interest, and talk of them
> with detail, minute, graphic, and accurate; but with
> them she rarely exchanged a word (Brontë, vi-vii).

Emily chose to seclude herself and to write about this seclusion as
an indulgence in Catherine. Emily also added an element of
pleasure through death in Catherine. She portrayed her living a life
where the only peace would be death. "[...] Catherine had an

unusual gloom in her aspect" (Brontë, 68). This gloom came from making the choice of being with Edgar Linton instead of Heathcliff. However, it also shows that there is nothing in Catherine's world that could truly make her happy. Emily lived her life in the same fashion. "[...] death appears more perfect than life; it stands ahead as the ultimate liberty and freedom" (Hardwick, 20). Death was the most perfect, peaceful interaction Emily and Catherine could ever wish for. The reasoning behind this notion is truly unknown. Yet, looking at the evidence, one might figure it stemmed from Branwell. Emily loved Branwell and wanted to protect him. "Emily Brontë took toward her brother an attitude of social pity and protectiveness" (Hardwick, 5). This attitude is also portrayed in Catherine. She loved Heathcliff and always wanted to protect him. "[...] if I marry Linton, I can aid Heathcliff to rise and place him out of my brother's power" (Brontë, 69). Catherine found her own way to protect Heathcliff, although it may not have worked. as where Emily found ways to protect Branwell, whether or not the outcome was good. At the end of volume one of

• • •

<u>Wuthering Heights</u>, Catherine dies, however, in real life Emily does not.

Figure 12: Cathryn Harrison as Cathy Linton; *A Reader's Guide to Wuthering Heights*

In volume two, or the second half, of *Wuthering Heights*, Catherine's daughter, who was born shortly before her death, becomes the next heroine of the book; Catherine Linton (Cathy), portrayed by Cathryn Harrison in the 1978 TV drama. Emily took advantage of Cathy and used her to portray her more playful, imaginary side. Cathy loved to pretend she was a part of the fairy world at Penistone Crags. She also created many other tales in which she acted out on the moors. "[...] that she often contrived to remain out from breakfast till tea; and then the evenings were spent in recounting her fanciful tales" (Brontë, 165). Cathy lived her tale and then told it to Nelly Dean. Where as Emily, lived her tale and then wrote about it with her sister, Anne. "Magical powers [...] became the common attributes [...] of [the] complex Glasstown Chronicles [which] evolved. [She] saw [herself] not circumscribed by the narrow limits of [her] home, but as carrying within [herself] powers that made [her] more than [a conqueror]" (Gérin, 15). This is how Emily spent most of her childhood, like the young Cathy. Emily- not only added her childish side to Cathy, but she also added her compassionate side to her as well. However, Emily, compassionate only towards Branwell, made Cathy compassionate only towards Linton Heathcliff, her cousin, at first. "[...] Catherine's displeasure softened into a perplexed sensation of pity and regret, largely blended with vague, uneasy doubts about Linton's actual circumstances, physical and social [...]" (Brontë, 227). After Linton's death, Cathy shows some compassion for

• • •
xxx

Hareton Earnshaw, her other cousin whom she used to pick on with Linton. Emily wrote Cathy to move her compassions from person to person while allowing her to learn the true meaning of death. Cathy gains this liberty that Emily already knows. "He's safe and I'm free, [...] you have left me so long to struggle against death, alone, that I feel and see only death! I feel like death!" (Brontë, 252). Here, Emily gives Cathy her last attribute, the appreciation for death. This is not the end of the complexity of Emily's characters or family members though. In fact, every character is graced with these gifts.

Figure 14: Morag Hood as Frances Earnshaw; *A Reader's Guide to Wuthering Heights*

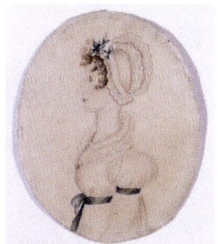

Figure 13: Maria Brontë; The Brontë Society

Emily may not have made any other characters strictly

based off of the people in her life however she touched each one with a piece of them. For example, Nelly Dean is based on her own servant and Catherine's mother, Frances Earnshaw, as portrayed by Morag Hood in the 1970 film, is like Emily's mother, Maria, both dying a few years after the birth of their last children.

> [...] one night, while leaning on his shoulder in the act of saying she thought she should be able to get up to-morrow, a fit of coughing took her - a very slight one - he raised her in his arms; she put her two hands about his neck, her face changed, and she was dead (Brontë, 55).

Not only did Emily's mother grace the pages of *Wuthering Heights*, but also her father. Patrick Brontë's stern yet loving character is in the veins of Hindley Earnshaw). "[...] for he had a kind heart, though he was rather sever some-times" (Brontë, 30). Patrick's attributes do not end here. Emily uses his illness in Edgar Linton's demise as portrayed by David Niven in the 1939 film. "He lay an image of sadness, and resignation, waiting his death" (Brontë, 242). Patrick and Edgar both start to go blind, become extremely ill, and Edgar dies of this illness. Emily created such fascinating characters because she used her real life to write the story. "The plot of *Wuthering Heights* is immensly complicated and yet there is the most felicitous union of author and subject" (Hardwick, 8). Many experts say that no one knows much about this beautiful heroine, however, when analyzing *Wuthering Heights*, one will learn more about Emily than any sibling could ever tell. This remains true for her poetry as well.

Figure 16: David Niven as Edgar Linton; *A Reader's Guide to Wuthering Heights*

Figure 15: Patrick Brontë; The Brontë Society

Emily wrote approximately two hundred and forteen poems

● ● ●

in her life time. She began writing around July 12th, 1836, or at least this was the earliest dated poem of hers was ever discovered. She tended to write with hymn-tune rhythms and used nature as her main vessel. "Emily's earliest poems have one point in common: They begin with a statement of nature's aspect, before the action or the dramatis personae, are introduced" (Gérin, 28). Half of Emily's poems are just poems written about life experiences and the other half are considered the "Gondal Chronicles" or "Gondal Sagas".

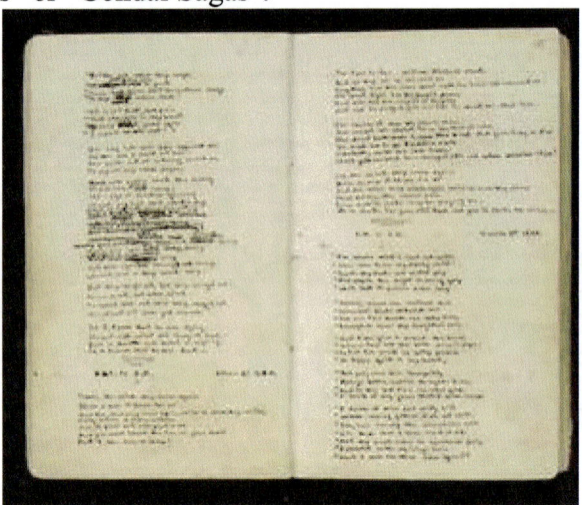

Figure 17: Pages of the Gondal Sagas

Some people might even conclude that all of Emily's poems are apart of the Chronicles considering the fact that the earliest

● ● ●

reference to these poems are in a diary entry made in 1834, and when publishing her book with her sisters, Emily changed some of the poems from the "Gondal Saga" so the reader did not read about a character, but a narrator instead. The full story of the "Gondal Chronicles" may be lost, but what was left behind proves that Emily enjoyed mixing reality with fiction and by exploring these poems, a great deal of Emily's life can be uncovered.

The "Gondal Chronicles" started when Emily, Anne, Charlotte, and Branwell played their imaginary games as children. It all came about when Branwell received those twelve wooden soldiers. It was 1826 when Charlotte created the Glasstown Confederacy. Each child ran his/her own island and country. However, Emily only played along for a year before she started getting tired of Charlotte's antics making Emily's country inferior to hers. It was 1827 when Emily convinced Anne to have a rebellion with her, breaking off from Charlotte and Branwell, creating the "Gondal Sagas". Emily and Anne enjoyed running around the moors as children, playing their imaginary game. "On the top of a moor or in a deep glen Emily was a child in spirit for glee and enjoyment ... A spell of mischief... lurked in her on occasions when out on the moors" (Nussey, 1871). Emily and Anne would spend the day running about their their imaginary world and the night recording all of their adventures. They began to form these adventures into poems when Emily was around sixteen years old. They used the nature around them as a muse for their poems. "It was as Emily and Anne roamed the moors as growing girls, learning more each day about the natural life about them, that the feeling for Gondal was born" (Gérin, 25). Once the "Gondal Sagas" were born, Emily and Anne took the story to great lengths.

Gondal was a country Emily and Anne created that was located in the South Pacific. It was a northern island covered in moorland and snow. They based it on Yorkshire. South of Gondal was another island they called Gaaldine. Gaaldine had a tropical climate and was subject to Gondal. Emily and Anne took their childhood games to new lengths. They did not just create a world that they desired, but they created characters who had real emotions. The beginning of the Gondal history follows Julius Brenzaida, a war-like man based on the Brontës' tales of Angria. Julius had two lovers, Rosina, who became his wife and queen, and Geraldine Sidonia, who was the mother of his child, Augusta Geraldine Almeda, dubbed A.G.A. Julius was a man who had a backstabbing personality. He befriended the king of Exina, Gerald, who he had a coronation with and then shortly after captured and executed him. During a civil war, Julius is murdered leaving his daughter, A.G.A., to succeed him. "Blood red, her rose, and narrow-straight, / His fierce beams struck my brow; / The soul of nature sprang, elate, / But mine sank sad and low!" (Brontë, STARS). A.G.A. is much like her father in temperment, having several lovers, and is murdered during a civil war. "`Twas the night her comrades gathered all / within their city's rock wall" (Brontë, GERALDINE). Her lovers consisted of Alexander of Elbë,

Fernando de Samara, and Alfred Sidonia of Aspen Castle. These men all die within the story as well.

Although truly fictional, the characters become alive because they are pieces of Emily and Anne. The whole picture is not just their personality and life, but the life they wished for.

> The Gondal Chronicles deal predominantly with a feminine and royalist world [....] It might also be deduced that it was because the poetry of Gondal was so close a reflection of their way of life and their most personal aspirations towards liberty that the plots remained so essentially feminine (Gerin, 26).

Emily wished for a world where she lay in the center. Emily kept this wish a secret from everyone except Anne. Anne shared the same secret with Emily, which is why their writtings were never shared with anyone. "Gondal was more than a childish invention; it was a way of life, which they shared in secret at each hour of every day" (Gérin, 25). Gondal may have been a secret the two sisters shared, but it was something that would not stay hidden for long.

Emily would write down her Gondal adventures in her downtime. She would also write other poems when she had no new Gondal infortmation to tell. In 1845, her secret notebook was discovered by Charlotte. She did not write to be read, but only to relieve a burdened heart.

> "One day," writes Charlotte in 1850, recollecting the near, vanished past, One day in autumn of 1845, I accidentally lighted in a manuscript volume of verse in my sister Emily's handwriting. Of course I was not surprised, knowing that she could and did write verse. I looked it over, and something more than surprise seized me, - a deep conviction that these were not common effusions, not at all like the poetry women generally write. I thought them condensed and terse, vigorous and genuine. To my

ear they also had a perculear music, wild,

melancholy and elevating (Robinson, 1612).

Emily was furious with Charlotte. She felt violated and betrayed by Charlotte's snooping. "My sister Emily was not a person of demonstrative character, nor one on the recesses of whose mind and feelings even those nearest and dearest to her could, with impunity, intrude unliscesened; it took hours to reconcile her to the discovery I had made, and days to persuade her that such poems merited publication" (Gérin, 182). Emily was not only rejecting her secrets being published, but she always rejected the servitude of careers and a fixed life. She felt that a career was the slavery of poorly paid work. However, she finally agreed to publish her poems in a book with Charlotte and Anne's poems as well. Emily choose only twenty one of her poems to be published. She considered these her non-Gondal poems. However, it has been noted that some of these poems do belong to the one hundred and ninty three poems in the chronicles; Emily simply removed the characaters' names. It took, what felt like, forever for the girls to find a publisher willing to take them on. In 1846, Messr's publishing was the company they choose to go with, not having much choice. "Ultimately the tree sisters found a publisher who would undertake the work upon commission [...]" (Robinson, 1785). The book was titled *The Poems of Currier, Ellis, and Acton Bell*. This was the first time the girls used their pseudonyms. Unfortunately, their book did not do so well. Athenoeum reviewed the book. He states, "[Ellis Bell is] a fine quaint spirit with an evident power of wing that may reach heights not here attempted" [...] The little book was evidentally a failure [...]" (Robinson, 1800). In the end, the book only sold two copies. This may have been quite discouraging to Emily, but it did not make her give up.

> There is no doubt about Emily's reserve, her hesitation about publication. Still it seems worthwhile to remember that she did help with the preparation of the book of poems and its failure did

not deter her from pressing on with her novel

Wuthering Heights nor from sending that to a

publisher and even writing him about her work on

another novel, never finished, and now lost

(Hardwick, 17-18).

Although she did not live to see it, *Wuthering Heights* eventually

succeeded in the literature community.

"It is Friday evening - near 9 o'clock - wild rainy weather, I am

seated in the diningroom alone - [...]" ~Emily Brontë's Diary Entry

- July 30, 1841

Before moving on to the death and downfall of Emily

Brontë, there is still much more to explore of her life and

personality. Emily lived her life alone, no companion or children to

succeed her. She dedicated her love and pure emotions to her

family, especially Branwell. This was a conscious decision she

made solely alone. "Emily Brontë appears in every way indifferent

to the need for love and companionship that tortured the lives of her sisters" (Harwick, 8). She watched her sisters' hearts break and had no desire to feel those human emotions herself. She used sympathy to feel what they were feeling. "The atmosphere of suffering and grief by her sisters gave Emily an insight into feelings which she would not have otherwise have known [...]" (Gérin, 173). Emily lived a double life from a world without to a world within. She had no need, no desire, no want for true companionship. Her fantasies were enough for her.

> The lack of romance in real life, the waste of refined feelings, the disillusion of tender hearts, these were subjects far more to her taste [....] To a girl with so reticent a nature, the revelation of her most secret experiences was wholly repugnant (Gérin, 179-184).

This explains why Emily's writings are so important; they were her gateway to the human emotion. However the only human emotion and experience Emily ever yearned for was death. "For Emily, religous fulfilment was to be found in the union of the individual spirit with the eternal spirits that she found in nature [...]" (The Brontë Parsonage Museum). Nature was always surrounding, and Emily felt that true life, emotion, and religous spirituality was being one with nature: in the ground dead. In all that she wrote and all that she said; she appears to be fascinated, obsessed, and wishing for death. "Emily's attitude to failure has crystalized years ago; in nature there was no such thing as success or failure, only suffering and death" (Gérin, 177). Little did Emily know, her spiritual wishes would come sooner than she had thought.

At the end of 1846, Emily stopped writing altogether. Whether it was the failure of her poetry book, the bad reviews for *Wuthering Heights*, or for some other reason, it is unknown. Although Emily did not die until 1848, 1846 seems to be the beginning of her demise. She threw herself into the role of mother and caretaker for her opium-eater brother. Branwell was the end for Emily. In the autumn of 1848, Branwell became extremely ill.

However, no doctor seemed to discover he was sick; they all felt it was just side effects from his alcoholism and opium use. "He was weak, certainly, and his appitite failed; but opium-eaters are not strong nor hungry" (Robinson, 2742). Although his drinking and drug habits led to the same symptoms of the cold he had, he really was in imminent danger. A few days prior to his death, Branwell took a trip to his friend's house. Mr. Grundy recalls this visit:

> Presently the door opened cautiously, and a head appeared. It was a mass of red, unkempt, uncut hair, wildly floating round a great, gaunt forhead; the cheeks yellow and hollow, the mouth fallen, the thin white lips not trembling but shaking, the sunken eyes, once small, now glaring with the light of madness - all told the sad tale but too surely [....] Another glass of brandy, brought him back to something like the Brontë of old. He even ate some dinner, a thing which he said he had not done for

long; so our last interview was pleasant though

grave [....] He described himself as waiting

anxiously for death - indeed, longing for it and

happy, in these his sane moments, to think it was so

near. He once again declared that that death would

be due to the story I knew, and to nothing else

(Robinson, 2763-2769).

After his visit, Branwell went home and on October 1, 1848, he

lived his last moments.

He insisted upon getting up; if he had succumbed to

the horrors of extinction; he would die as he thought

no one had ever died before, standing. So, like some

ancient Celtic hero, when the last agony began, he

rose to his feet; hushed and awe-sticken, the old

father, praying Anne, loving Emily, looked on. He

rose to his feet and died erect after twenty minutes'

• • •

struggle (Robinson, 2792).

The doctors claimed his death being for consumption. This was the beginning of the end for Emily. She went to Branwell's funeral, returned home, and never left again.

Emily came down with a cough and cold herself. Charlotte, at first notice, wanted Emily to see a doctor; Emily refused. Since Branwell was gone and no one else seemed to rely on her, Emily found no reason to live anymore.

> She took her brother's death very much to
> heart, growing thin and pale and saying
> nothing [....] For after his funeral, she never
> rallied, a cold and cough taken then,
> gained fearful hold upon her [....] Emily who
> had cheerfully devoted herself to Branwell.
> He being dead, the motive of her life seemed
> gone (Robinson, 2800-2818).

● ● ●

However, shortly after Emily's illness had started, Charlotte, Anne, and her father, Patrick, fell ill. Emily found another reason for living. She needed to take care of her family.

> Emily would not give up. She felt herself doubly necessary to the household in this hour of trail [....] Emily, who had always been relied upon for strength and courage and endurance, should show herself unworthy of the trust when she was most sorely needed; that she, so inclined to take all the duties on herself, so necessary to the daily managment of the house, should throw up her charge in the moment of trail, cast away her arms in the moment of battle, and give her fellow sufferers the extra burden of her weakness; such a thing was impossible to her (Robinson, 2837).

Emily continued to nurse her family back to health. She refused, no matter how sick she was, to be waited on. She continued her daily tasks as if nothing was wrong with her. Emily's illness lasted for months; the illness started to inflame her lungs. Charlotte explains the seriousness of Emily's illness in a letter on October 29, 1848. She wrote,

> I feel much more uneasy about my sister than myself just now. Emily's cold and cough are very obstinate. I fear she has a pain in her chest, and I sometimes catch a shortness in her breathing when she has moved at all quickly. She looks very thin and pale. Her reserved nature occasions me great uneasiness of mind. It is useless to question her; you get no answer. It is still more useless to recommend remedies; they are never adopted (Robinson, 2829).

Charlotte grew more and more concerned about Emily. She begged her again to see a doctor; Emily once again refused. Time moved by quickley as Emily's cold grew worse. It was November 29, 1848, When Charlotte wrote Ellen again about Emily,

> I told you Emily was ill in my last letter. She has not rallied yet. She is very ill. I believe if you were to see her your impression would be that there is no hope [....] Her pulse, the only time she allowed it to be felt, was found to beat 115 per minute. In this state she resolutely refuses to see a docor. She will give no explanation of her feelings; she will scarcely allow her feelings to be alluded to (Robinson, 2856).

Charlotte pushed again for Emily to see a doctor. Emily, again, refused. Charlotte decided to take matters into her own hands and wrote a letter to a doctor describing Emily's aliments. The doctor sent a bottle of medicine for Emily. He felt no need to go out to the house; speculation says he felt the cause was hopeless. Charlotte attempted to give the medicine to Emily, however she refused to take it.

> Did Emily wish to die? We cannot know. But if, as
> appears all too probable from the signs of her
> sorrow, her visions had deserted her, her pursuit of
> them beyond death could explain her rejection of
> life as her poems had always shown. Emily had
> divided views on death. At one time it had appeared
> to her as the most desirable consummation that
> existence had to offer [...] (Gérin, 252).

December came and Emily grew worse. Her life became a horrible
contradiction of fear and hope on a daily basis. Starting around
December 14, 1848, Emily began to have falling spells.
"Nevertheless she persisted in rising, dressing herself alone, and
doing everything for herself" (Robinson, 2878). These spells
continued until her last day. It was December 19, 1848 when
Emily finally came to her senses and decided to see a doctor. It
was around two o'clock when Anne and Charlotte pleaded with

Emily to go lie down in bed and rest. Emily refused knowing there was nothing more that anyone could do, but she still asked for the doctor. "She could no longer speak, but - gasping ina huskey whisper - she said, if you send for a doctor I will see him now" (Robinson, 2892). Emily then tried to get up from the couch and walk away, but she was too weak and in that moment Emily received her wish: she was dead. Dr. Wheelhouse, the family doctor, never made it to Emily in time for her death, but was the man to pronounce her dead. He stated the cause of death to be from "Consumption - 2 months' duration" (Gérin, 259). Emily is buried inside Haworth Parish Church in Haworth, Yorkshire.

Figure 18: Inside Haworth Parish Church in Haworth, Yorkshire; Poet's Grave

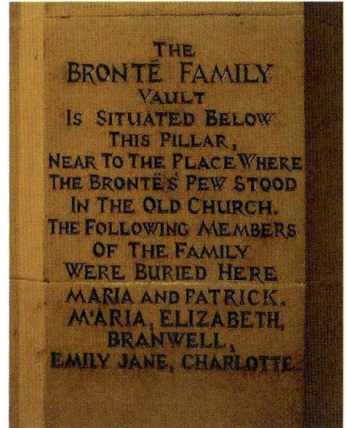

**Figure 19: The Brontë Family Vault;
Poet's Grave**

Her tombstone reads the "last lines" she ever wrote:

No coward soul is mine,

No trembler in the world's storm - troubled sphere;

I see heaven's glories shine,

And faith shines equal, arming me from fear.

• • •

O God, within my breast,

Almighty, ever-present Deity!

Life, that in me has rest,

As I - undying life - have power in Thee.

Vain are the thousand creeds

That move men's hearts: unutterably vain,

Worthless as withered weeds,

Or idlest froth amid the boundless main,

To waken doubt in one

Holding so fast by thine infinity;

So surely anchored on

The steadfast rock of immortality.

With wide-embracing love

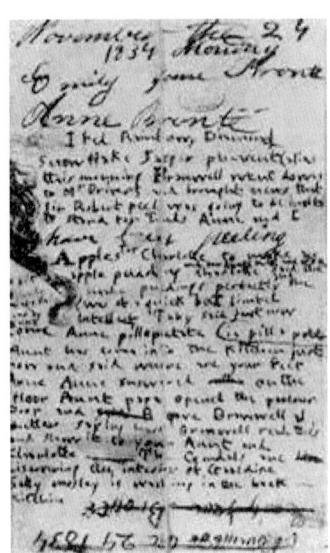

Thy spirit animates eternal years,

Figure 20: Emily's Diary

Pervades and broods above,

Changes, sustains, dissolves, creates and rears.

Though earth and man were gone,

And suns and universes ceased to be,

And Thou wert left alone,

Every existence would exist in Thee.

There is not room for Death,

No atom that his might could render void;

Thou - Thou are being, breath,

And what Thou art may never be destroyed.

Emily Brontë honorably seized her talents and in this she was heroic. All that is to be discovered about Emily is found in the only writtings of hers that have survived. This includes six letters from her birthday letters, diary entries, and letters to Ellen Nussey, her novel *Wuthering Heights*, and her poems. The rest to be discovered came from her sisters, Charlotte and Anne. When placing these items under a microscope, it is to be found that Emily was a wild woman who cared more about her family than herself. She wrote about what she knew, mixing reality with her fantasies, allowing every reader to discover Emily Brontë: A real life heroine.

Figure 23: Drawing by Emily

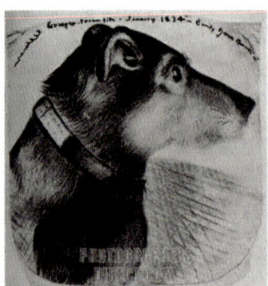

Figure 22: Drawing by Emily

Figure 21: Drawing by Emily

Figure 24: Emily Brontë; The Brontë Society

Works Cited

Alexander, Christine. *Tales of Glass Town, Angria, and Gondal: Selected Writings*. Oxford University Press, Oxford, England 2010.

An Emily Brontë Chronology. http://www.lang.nagoya-u.ac.jp/~matsuoka/Bronte-Emily-Chro.html

Benvenuto, Richard. *Emily Brontë*. Twayne Publishers, 1982.

Birrell, A. *The Life of Charlotte Brontë*. Walter Scott, London, 1887.

Brontë, Anne, Brontë, Charlotte, and Brontë, Emily. *The Poems by Currier, Ellis, and Acton*

Bell. Kindle Edition, 2003.

Brontë, Charlotte. *"A History of the Year"*, BPM, London, 1829.

Brontë, Emily. *Wuthering Heights*. Barnes and Noble INC., USA 1993.

Brontë Letters and Diary Papers.

http://www.academic.brooklyn.cuny.edu/english/melani/novel_19c/wuthering/diary_papers#diary

Chadwick, Ellis. *In the Footsteps of the Brontë's*. Pitman, London, 1914.

Cousin, John W. *A Short Biographical Dictionary of English Literature*. J.M. Dent and Sons

LTD., 1910, Kindle Edition, 2003.

Emily Jane Brontë.

http://www.bookandwriters.co.uk/writer/B/emily-jane-bronte.asp

Gérin, Winifred. *Emily Brontë*. Oxford University Press, Oxford, England, 1978.

Glaskell, E. *Life of Charlotte Brontë*. 2 Vols., Smith, Elder: 3rd Ed.,

London, Sept. 1857.

Hardwick, Elizabeth. *Seduction and Betrayal: Women and Literature*. Random House Inc., New York, 1975.

Hewish, J. *Emily Brontë: A Critical and Biographical Study*. Macmillan, London, 1969.

Hinkley, Laura. *The Brontë's: Charlotte and Emily*. Hammond, London, 1945.

Mackay, Angus M. *The Brontë's: Fact and Fiction*. Service and Paton, London, 1897.

Moore, Virginia. *The Life and Eager Death of Emily Brontë*. Rich and Cowan, London, 1936.

Mott, Joan, and Brown, Helen. *Gondal Poems*. Blackwell, Oxford, England, 1938.

Nussey, E. "Reminiscences of Charlotte Brontë". *Scribner's*

Magazine, England, May 1871.

Robinson, Mary F. *Emily Brontë*. W.H. Allen and Co., 1883, Kindle Edition, 2000.

Self, Cameron. *Emily Brontë*. 2003.
http://www.poetsgrave.co.uk/bronte.htm

Shorter, C.K. *The Brontë's: Life and Letters*. Hodder and Stoughton, London, 1908.

Sinclair, May. *The Three Brontë's*. Hutchinson, London, 1912.

The Brontë Parsonage Museum and Brontë Society.

http://www.bront-45657-001.dsrv.co.uk/index.php

The Reader's Guide to Emily Brontë's "Wuthering Heights"

http://www.wuthering-heights.co.uk

Visick, Mary. *The Genesis of Wuthering Heights*. Hong Kong

University Press, China, 1958.

Williams, Oscar, ed. *Master Poems of the English Language.*

Washington Square Press, NY, NY, 1967.

8907125R00036

Printed in Great Britain
by Amazon.co.uk, Ltd.,
Marston Gate.